The Positive Solution to a Negative Workplace

Susie Stone

Some names and identifying details have been changed to protect the privacy of individuals. The methods described within this book are the author's personal thoughts. They are not intended to be a definitive set of instructions for this project. You may discover there are other methods and materials to accomplish the same end result. If you wish to apply ideas contained in this book, you are taking full responsibility for your actions.

e-book cover and dust jacket created and designed by
pro_ebookcovers at fiverr.com

Createspace editions:

ISBN: 1537022857
ISBN-13: 97815307022857

DEDICATION

This book is dedicated to the employees that walked through the fire with me. To the ones who re-assured me I wasn't crazy, to the ones who listened and cared. But it is also dedicated to the others. To the staff, managers, and anyone else that ever heard me say, "have a good evening" or "thank you." I was sincere. I loved you all and it is my greatest wish that you have a fantastic life.

But most of all, it's for Gamer and Red. I love you to the breakroom and back.

CONTENTS

INTRODUCTION

In 1999, I landed my dream job with a company that had great values, a bright future, and compassion for its employees. I loved my work, even during tough periods (all jobs have tough situations). I was known as one of the best and brightest in my district and was promoted quickly. I was a go-to manager that could be counted on.

Fast forward fourteen years. I was in a new region and unrecognizable by my previous peers and bosses. My friends and family were concerned for my health and wellbeing. When I walked out of the front doors of my company for the final time, I wept openly, not because I was sad for leaving a job and co-workers that I loved. I wept because I felt like the weight of the entire building was lifted off my soul. For the next few months, I would have nightmares where I was told I still had my job and needed to go into work.

I began to spend time reflecting how I went from a positive, upbeat person who was damn good at her job to the broken negative being that stopped trying to make things better and starting spending their time figuring out how to just make it through the day. My workplace was a den of backbiting, gossip, manipulation, and fear. The management above me was anti-company, inappropriate, and offensive. My boss manipulated others for their own amusement, openly favored some over others, and on at least one occasion used company mail to send sexual items to another manager at another branch, bragging about it all the while. I would use any gossip I could find as a commodity to exchange for favor with this manager because if you didn't have their favor, you were sunk. At the next level up was another boss that was just as inappropriate and offensive. This boss would refer to other employees with degrading nicknames, ignore scheduled appointments, and stop what they were doing to openly focus on and stare at attractive members of the opposite sex, sometimes in mid-sentence.

I allowed myself to become a reflection of all that was bad around me. I became just like them. I did not take actions available to me for fear of retribution, despite having strong “company policies” against any such action. It took its toll and I paid the price.

This program is built from my time reflecting on what I could have and should have done during the last horrible years with that company. Most of the steps and actions were known to me during my slide into becoming one of the negative people. I already had the knowledge and skills, I just didn’t use them. I honestly believe that if I had followed these steps, taken these actions, I wouldn’t have allowed myself to get to a point of having nightmares and being miserable. It is my fondest wish and desire that this program helps people before they get to that point.

If ***The Positive Solution to a Negative Workplace*** helps even one person for the better, I will consider it all worth it.

Peace.

1 The Toolbox

While you can influence those around you, you cannot control them. In truth, the only person you have control over is you. And, let's be honest, sometimes we all have situations that make it hard, if not impossible, to keep that personal control. So when it seems like the whole world needs an attitude adjustment, I suggest starting with yourself. And no, this won't necessarily be easy. Adjusting your attitude is a skill and even if you have used it in the past, skills take time to master and then you must practice to keep that mastery. But master this skill and make it a habit, and your life just got easier.

As with every job, using the correct tool can help you solve problems. Let's take a look inside the toolbox.

Toolbox Contents:

- Identify players
- Determine the limit
- Respond rather than react
- Identify what you can control
- Keep it private
- Attitude is a choice

Identify the Players

Ever return to work from a vacation or extended time off to find that you notice things you've never seen before? It's natural that we don't notice details that we see day after day or behaviors in people that we are so accustomed to, we hardly notice them at all. You can develop this same sense of clarity without using any time off. This involves making a list of everyone you work for and with in your daily environment. This list should be considered very private and for your eyes only. Make sure you do not make this list on a company computer or even in your workspace. Grab a notepad and take a moment at home, away from the job, and keep your list there once you make it. The best computer hacker in the world cannot access a legal pad on your kitchen table.

Start with a name (this can be in any order) and list your thoughts about this person. Do you hate them? Love them? Are they your work best friend? Do they gossip? Do they steal your ideas, manipulate others, sit quietly in the corner during lunch? You get the idea. Be honest with yourself; remember no one else is going to see this list. List all the great things as well as any negative things and listen to your intuition, making sure you note if you're just not sure how you feel as well. Make sure that you list any negative qualities in your work friends as well as good qualities in the ones you don't like.

Now in the left hand margin, mark the names of those that seem to cause the most friction at work. Give them a star or a little flag, anything to distinguish those from the coworkers who cause little or no friction in the workplace. Then count them up and note the number. Now count the number of names of those coworkers that don't cause you friction and put that number next to your first count. Hopefully you're non-friction co-workers will outnumber the ones that do, but if that's not the case, know you are not alone.

Go back to your list and re-read what you have written. Do any of the ones that cause you friction have what you feel are undesirable qualities or are manipulators? Do any of the ones that cause you no friction have somewhat nasty tendencies towards others? None of this is new information to you, but it may help you see others in a new light, or confirm or deny suspicions.

Try to see your list with your new awareness over the next few days and then come back to your list. See if there are any changes you might like to make. If there are quite a few, I suggest making a new list in the same manner and evaluating things again. You may even want to do this exercise several times over the next few weeks as you implement this program so that you can go back and compare your attitudes towards these people.

Determine the Limit

Learn to recognize when you are reaching your limit. Extreme frustration and conflict can push even the best people to do or say things they regret later. Chances are you have a high level of frustration quite a lot because you bought this book. Recognize that you are taking action to improve your work life. Sometimes just knowing that you are taking action to make things better can reduce this frustration level.

Make a scale in your head from one to ten, one being the absolute worst you can think of (for instance, losing your cool and saying or doing something that results in immediate termination) and with ten being the best day ever at work. Think about past incidents of extreme conflict or frustration and place them on that mental scale. Now think of that scale as a stoplight. Think of anything below a 3 as red, 3-7 as yellow, and 7-10 as green. Maybe you have more green light days than yellow, but chances are you have more yellow lights than red. As you work this program, and you see an improvement, you may find that you can reduce the scale of your yellow lights to a 4-7.

Implement this scale in situations at work. Recognize the level of your frustration so that you can see the level of control you have in reacting to work situations. Being able to rank and sort out your emotions can give you more power over yourself and work situations. Make sure you rank the good situations as well as the bad.

Respond vs. React

When we are in a highly charged environment or situation, we often react to things rather than respond to them. What's the difference? Reactions are quick, usually emotionally charged, and can often be off the cuff and uncontrolled. Responses are sometimes slower (the longer your practice responding rather than reacting, the timing will speed up) and are thought through and deliberate. An easy way to picture the difference is to look at the following scenario:

A small child wanders away from their parents and falls off a pier into the water as a crowd watches in horror. One man reacts by jumping into the water below and swimming to the child. The rescue squad responds by jumping into the rescue truck, turning on sirens, and making their way to the pier. When the rescue squad arrives, they assist pulling the child and the man out of the frigid waters and checking them for injuries. The news asks the man why he chose to save the child and the man answers, "I didn't even think about it."

The man in the scenario reacted (without thinking) and the rescue squad responded (doing their job.) Reactions are not always bad, sometimes reactions can be very good things, especially in life threatening situations. However, in work culture, responses are better most of the time.

Try to consciously remember to respond rather than react. Remember if you've been in a highly charged environment for a good length of time, this is a skill you will have to remember to use.

Identify What You Can Control:

Here are two things you have absolute, complete control over:

1. The thoughts in your head
2. Behavior you exhibit

Don't feel like you have complete control over these two things? You are not alone. Our daily lives are made up out of habits, repetition, familiarity, and rituals. When you brush your teeth, do you change the order of operations? Maybe, if you were engaged in deep thoughts, you might have put the toothbrush in your mouth without any toothpaste by accident. But the majority of the time you do things in the exact same manner. You probably put on your shoes the exact same way every day. If you drive a stick shift car, do you just drive or do you consciously push in the clutch and shift from first to second? If you've driven a stick shift for any length of time, chances are it's completely on autopilot as far as shifting goes. Our thoughts and behaviors are exactly the same.

When you have been caught up in negative thinking, self-doubt, anger, or fearful thoughts, it can be very hard to change your thoughts. It's a skill. You have to actively monitor (you can do it, I promise!) your own thoughts and when you find the old pattern, deliberately shift gears in your thoughts. No one else is inside your head, you must learn to identify and change your own thought patterns.

If you have been finding yourself in exhibiting negative behaviors, like gossiping, backbiting, or speaking without thinking things through (reacting rather than responding), you can change these things as well. The first step is to recognize that you are exhibiting a specific behavior, take responsibility for it, and deliberately changing that behavior, even if you are half-way through it.

This self-control is a skill. Skills take time and practice. Sure, there are people who have a natural talent for this self-control, and you may have had it at one time. But even those with natural talent need some sort of training. By recognizing and taking action by switching thoughts and behaviors, you will be training yourself to accept the control that you have over yourself.

You must also identify the other things in your job that you control. Do you set your own hours? Deadlines? Work environment? When you feel completely overwhelmed, ask yourself exactly what you have control over in the situation. Sometimes you may need to take out a piece of paper and make a list of these items. If something is completely out of your control, such as a deadline or customer's crazy requests, recognize that. See what it is that you cannot control and see what you can. So many times we feel as if we have no control at all, but remember, you have the power to control your own thoughts and actions!

Keep It Private

When you first begin working this program, I highly suggest that you keep it to yourself, at least in the work environment. Once you find things changing for the better, or co-workers start noticing a positive change in the things you do or ask you how you became so much happier at work, evaluate before telling them. If you announce to the breakroom or even your close work friends that you are trying to change your happiness level at work, it can lead it them thinking you have a problem with them. As you work further through the program, you may find out that some of the people you bonded with and trusted aren't necessarily good for you or what you thought they were, so do yourself a favor and keep it private for a while.

Keeping it private does not hinder you from removing yourself from uncomfortable situations where you have the control to remove yourself. If you find yourself engaging in an old negative behavior, say gossip at the break room coffee pot, you may be tempted to say something along the lines of "Wow. I'm going to really try and stop being so negative." This sometimes makes your co-workers feel like you are being nasty to them and it gets even more complicated if you trigger any guilt inside their own thoughts. Try suddenly "remembering something" or otherwise disengage without a conflict. (Not all conflict is bad, and we will deal with this later in the program.)

Attitude is a Choice

Remember that compartment in the toolbox where you keep the items you can control? Reach into that compartment and use your thoughts to change your attitude. Yes, attitude is a choice. That doesn't mean that you won't be disappointed at times. This doesn't mean that you won't be angry when someone else takes credit for your work. This doesn't mean that you won't be unhappy if there is a sudden demand for you to work on Saturday and you have coveted sporting event tickets. You are human. What this means is that you can learn to consciously choose how you view a situation. If it is a situation that you absolutely positively cannot change, you will only make yourself (and those around you) more miserable by displaying a miserable attitude. And if you're already surrounded by people with these attitudes, why would you throw gasoline upon the fire?

You do not have to be the sunny, happy go lucky person all the time. In fact, if you were pretty open about your unhappiness at work and you suddenly go 180 degrees, you may find yourself open to some pretty wild speculation. But you don't have to be a victim to your own bad attitude either. Recognize it, think about it, respond to it, and then choose your attitude. And when it comes time to choose your attitude, choose one that is at least pleasant to live with. Remember, it's going to be living in your head!

Remember:

- List the players
- Determine your limits
- Practice responding rather than reacting
- Identify what is in your control
- Keep it private
- Choose your thoughts and attitudes

2 Sharing Isn't Always Caring

The Quiet Start

Herd mentality, group thought, peer pressure, call it what you will, groups of people tend to follow trends and influence each other for good and not so good. Peers at work can be as cliquish as middle school girls. Sometimes people are so reluctant to see changes they want to make for themselves, they unintentionally (or even intentionally) sabotage one's quest for change.

Consider the plight of the dieter. One worker in the office decides to go on a diet. They're feeling motivated and have a program in place. Perhaps their doctor has told them that it is simply a must. Maybe they just want to look and feel better. They're focused on this change, but dieting can be hard and almost impossible for some people. So their focus is such that they share their plans with everyone. The next morning, the dieter walks into the breakroom to find donuts on the table. Now, maybe the dieter has no problem with these donuts and is able to walk away. Maybe the dieter eats a donut and fails. Let's look at how the donuts got there. Did someone just want donuts and brought some to share? Was someone happy that they weren't on a diet and decided to celebrate? The donuts could be a coincidence, a treat sent from a supplier without regard to any office politics. But maybe the donuts are from a passive aggressive peer.

The Story of the Nerds

An assistant manager, let's call him Doug, once announced that he was going to give up sugar as a group sat chatting before the weekly meeting. Doug said he knew it would be tough, but that he'd already stopped adding it to his coffee and he was almost accustomed to the new taste. The branch manager sat quietly, waiting for the rest of the group. When those already in attendance started giving Doug lots of praise and attention, the branch manager began to fidget and scowl. I asked the manager if there was a problem, and she dismissed me with a curt, "No, why would there be a problem?"

The next day, the manager came into work with a giant glass jar. I watched as she placed it on the breakroom table and filled it with tiny boxes of Nerds candy.

"You know those are Doug's favorite candy, right?" I asked.

"I know."

"Don't you think that's a little mean?" I asked.

"It's not my problem if he gave up sugar," she replied as she smiled and went to her office.

In case you are wondering, I don't know if Doug ever ate a box of those Nerds. He did ask me if I knew where they had come from and I told him. I do know that I made a mental note about the meanness of the incident and considered her a truly bad apple from that point on.

The Quest for Change

Now consider your quest for change. If you talk about your desire to change at work, how will your peers react? If you tell your work acquaintances that you are tired of negativity and you won't stand for it, how will they feel? Will they feel like you are being passive aggressive by telling them that they're being negative? While you are giving yourself distance to regroup, you don't want complete alienation from your team mates. You just need some space to create a barrier between yourself and the negativity of your work environment. This will allow you to see the patterns of your coworkers and make positive changes to yourself so that you are immune to those behaviors.

It would be best to start quietly, without sharing. Get a few changes under your belt and allow yourself some time to get your program in place. After a week or two, look at your co-workers with the new perspective you have gained giving yourself some space and a break from negativity. Go back to your Toolbox list identifying the players and see if you need to reclassify anyone. You may find that your most sympathetic ear is the most vicious, sly gossip in the company.

Not all herd mentality is deliberately viscous. But sometimes there is a fine line between small personal changes and rocking the boat. If you're trying to throw yourself a life line, don't tie it to a shark.

Remember:

- Recognize herd mentality
- Not everyone will be supportive
- Consider peer reaction
- Start quietly
- Use your Toolbox

3 Unsocial Media

Life in the digital age allows us constant, continual contact with the world around us and the world far, far away. This can bring us great joy and solidify old friendships and family relations. Twitter allows us to connect to people we would never connect with in real life, like when a celebrity or author responds to your tweet. Facebook is multigenerational and can allow us to celebrate occasions with those who are physically too far away to socialize with in person. Instagram allows us to see pictures of new babies as well as beautiful shots of the earth taken by astronauts on the International Space Station. And while texting is considered a social media by some (it is a form of communication through a digital interface) and not by others (it is not seen by multiple people in a public setting), it will be included here in this section. And these are just a few examples of social media available in our lives.

So what happens when you are in a negative mindset and you indulge in social media? Well, much like real, unplugged life, it depends on who you hang out with. If you surround yourself with positive people who lift you up, you will feel these effects. If you surround yourself with negative people, you will find yourself spiraling down the rabbit hole.

Should you just unfriend, unfollow, and block out those negative Nancys? Well, yes and no. What you have to do is put them in their place. I have many friends that I love and I like knowing what happens in their life, but maybe they post too much or have a political stance that goes directly against everything I believe. I don't like being bombarded by them, but I like connecting with them on my own terms. When I go see what Hannah is doing, I know that I'm going to see political memes dominate her posts and when I check on Grace, I know that I will see everything she has eaten in the last few days.

Social Media- Incoming

Facebook is by far the easiest of the social networking sites to control your own news feed. They have settings that allow you to sort your friends into acquaintances, work place colleagues, close friends, and family. These are in your left hand sidebar on your Facebook homepage. They're easy to set up and I highly recommend it. Get all those work people into one place. Round the family up and classify them. Sort out your close friends so people that make you feel good are at your fingertips. And those negative Nancys? Unfollow them. Yes, you can unfollow someone without unfriending them and they'll never know. For information on how to do these things, simply visit the Help Center on Facebook and search for *Controlling What You See In News Feed.*

Another potential trap in Facebook can be the chat/messenger feature. On the bottom right of the chat bar, you will find your options button. Clicking on it and selecting *Advance Options* will allow you to customize who sees that you are available to chat and who doesn't. Utilize this feature so that chat/messenger interactions add only a positive value to your Facebook experience.

LinkedIn is a valuable social media platform that many

erroneously consider "Facebook for work." It is a valuable tool for recruitment, job seeking, and networking. You should keep your LinkedIn profile and network professional and positive. There is more information about LinkenIn in Chapter 10.

Twitter is different as you aren't actually friending people or businesses, you are following them. Simply unfollow the users that bring down your positive vibrations and unless their account is private, you can check in on what they have to say whenever you feel like it. Likewise to businesses or brands that you love but seem to bombard your account with the same tweet over and over. Don't feel like you have to follow an account just because they follow you. Follow only those whose content enrich your life.

Now that you have your news feed happier, whenever you feel like checking in on the political negative Nancy, you can brace yourself to look between the memes and find the personal news and tidbits. You can check on a foodie when you've just finished off a good meal. You can check on a braggart and like all the pictures of their kids accepting their billion dollar scholarships when the mood strikes you right. Above all, make sure your news feed in enriching your life. It should be a happy place, and you can make it so.

Social Media- Outgoing

Most everyone is familiar with the adage of "You are what you eat." The same theory can be applied to what you speak. You don't have to believe in the Law of Attraction or be a hippie guru to follow this advice. Robert K. Merton, a sociologist, is credited with coining the term Self-Fulfilling Prophecy back in 1947. If you've never heard the term, you may be more familiar with the example of Self-Fulfilling Prophecy called The Placebo Effect.

Posting positive items and status updates will help you achieve a positive outlook. But, by all means, don't be insincere. You can post all the I CAN! happy memes in the world, but when you treat other people nasty or the next post is nothing but complaint after complaint, the sincerity will be lost.

Complaining about work can be a particular nasty habit and most companies have some sort of digital policy covering what you can and can't say about your company or coworkers. Certainly sales figures or other confidential company information should be off limits. But most of all don't put out the self-fulfilling prophecy of a status along the lines of: Off to have a crappy day at work. Dishing gossip about co-workers is never a good idea. Remember if you wouldn't say it in person, don't put it on Facebook. Likewise, avoid mentioning that you may be looking for another job unless you want your boss or co-workers to know about it.

Hopefully your digital social landscape is now a happier place that welcomes you when you check in and you think twice before posting that status update and make sure it's what you want the world to see.

Texts from work

Some people have a love/hate relationship with the text message. On one hand, it's very convenient to dash off a question or hello that is not time sensitive. Perhaps the person to whom you wish to communicate with is at dinner, or in a meeting, or hanging with their family, you can send off that message and when the person finds it convenient, they can reply at their leisure. On the other hand, some find texts to be cold and impersonal. These days texting can be a blessing and a curse, and this is especially true with texts from co-workers and bosses.

The Serial Texter/Caller

My last boss was a serial texter. She didn't care that you were out with family for Grandma's 90th birthday or in the ER with your sick child, she would text you. Chances are you will encounter a serial texter from work at some point in your career. Recognizing this can be half the battle and some little tips and tricks can help you maintain some sanity and order on your smart phone.

Most smartphones have privacy settings that allow the person texting you to see if your text has been delivered or read. Change that setting so that it only shows "delivered." This buys you time to digest and respond on your time table.

Remember that texts are not necessarily secure communications. One co-worker I knew left his smartphone in a communal workspace during the day and his privacy settings allowed at least part of any text messages to appear on his screen, even if his phone was locked. Another coworker would just help themselves with any unlocked phone. Often people can be tempted to read over the shoulder when someone else is texting in their area. When you send a text, always assume that someone other than the recipient will read it. That simple rule can help avoid many headaches.

The frequency of calls and texts outside of normal work hours is often an office wide accepted culture. Some workplaces rarely do it; others survive (and maybe even thrive) on these types of communications. If your phone is provided through work, there isn't much you can do about it. But if the phone is your own, and you're not in position to be an emergency contact for the building or other authority figure, you can control if you answer your calls or texts. I have one friend who keeps her landline just for this reason. She lets it be known that in emergencies, she is happy to be reached at her home landline telephone number and that otherwise, she turns her cell phone off at a certain time each night. I know that my last serial texter boss would never pick up the phone to call with her passive aggressive style of communication because the communication would've been two way instead of the one direction that she so dearly loved.

So take back your social media. Technology should aid and enrich our lives, not make it miserable. Make your news feeds a positive, supportive network and make it fun again.

Remember:

- Recognize the impact of social media
- Control your news feed
- Sort friends into categories
- Unfollow as necessary
- Unfriend if needed
- Clean other social media feeds
- Monitor what you post
- Change smartphone privacy settings
- Consider texts as public communications

4 Breaking the Break

Consider your time at work, *all* of your time at work. Most people think of their time at work as the time spent manning their workstation, in meetings, or engaged with clients. But work really goes beyond the time you actively work. Negativity breeds during these times. So what about the times when you are at work, but not actively working?

Lunchtime

How do you spend your lunch? Do you have a regular meal? A regular partner? Do you leave or utilize a company breakroom or cafeteria? If you've been at your job for a significant amount of time, chances are you have a set routine for your lunch. Many workers find themselves eating at their desk, or on the fly during the day so that they can spend their lunch break working. Whatever you do for lunch every day, change it.

Lunch breaks can be a minefield if you already feel like you work in a hostile environment. Some companies are all lip service when it comes to breaks. What your HR representative tells you when you are hired can be a completely different scenario when you're on the job. You may find yourself thinking, "What happened to my hour lunch mentioned in the employee handbook?" Lunch breaks can be tricky. If everyone in the office routinely takes less time than allotted, you run the risk of being seen as an outsider if you take the full break. Being mindful about what is acceptable in your office can make your breaks a little less stressful.

See which of these actions can help you feel a little more like you've had a break:

- Take your lunch break away from the office. You could grab a bite to eat in a café, restaurant, or fast food establishment. If you prefer to bring your own food from home, try a nearby park, or your car. Sometimes the simple act of leaving work premises for a little while can help refresh your mind and soul.
- Having lunch with a work friend? A gentle suggestion to leave work at work and a little redirection of conversation, if needed, can help avoid any lunch time complaint sessions.
- Invite the newbie. If you have a new co-worker, inviting them to dine with you can help foster a positive relationship. Just make sure you aren't filling their head with all the work problems that lead you to this program. A fresh perspective can sometimes be just what the doctor ordered.
- If your meals are confined to a break room or cafeteria or you just feel as if you cannot leave, try the iPod trick. A pair of earbuds can signal to others that you are not open for conversation and music is a great mood changer. Consider how you want to feel when your break is over when choosing your playlist. Do you want to be relaxed? Energized? An audio book can allow you to leave the building into another world while waiting on your turn at the microwave. Maybe listen to a motivational speaker give a TED talk on your smartphone. Whatever you choose, just

remember to be mindful that overly loud earbuds can damage your hearing as well as annoy others.

- Bring a book. Even if you haven't read a book since your school days, pick up a new one and start new habit. Fiction or non-fiction, it doesn't matter. Books can transport you to other worlds or teach new skills. Just be mindful that marking up a copy of ***Resumes for Dummies*** can and will lead your coworkers to speculation, so choose your title wisely or use an e-reader. A pair of earbuds (even if they aren't playing anything) can aid in getting solitude out of your book.
- If you often find yourself running errands during your lunch break, consider limiting it to just once or twice a week. You may be saving time at your own expense.

Small Breaks, Big Changes

Taking small breaks throughout the day can help clear your mind, reduce stress, and make you more productive if they are kept positive. Too often, a little gossip around the coffee pot or water cooler can add to larger negativity problems.

If your office takes routine ten or fifteen minute breaks try these:

- Games such as Sudoku or a crossword puzzle, which require you to focus and concentrate on them. Putting pen to paper is better than the smart phone or tablet screen, but those games can be beneficial as long as you aren't playing on your work computer screen.
- Text a quick hello (no nagging about non-work issues or honey do lists) to your significant other, kids, best friend, mom, or other loved one to remind them that you are thinking of them and wishing them a good day.
- Close your eyes and try a ten minute guided meditation.
- Take a brisk walk to get your blood pumping, outside if possible.

- Eat! A nutritious snack can change your attitude and your day. Just beware that a sugar crash can hurt a positive mood.

Here are some unofficial breaks that you can do during the day, often while you're being productive:

- Do 10 neck rolls, five each direction, several times a day.
- Perform shoulder shrugs, really big ones pressing up and down.
- Take 10 really big, really deep breaths.
- Try the Seventh Inning Stretch! About an hour and a half before the end of your work day, stand up and stretch your hands over your head as you rise on your tippy toes. Throw in some side to side body twists and some toe or knee touches before sitting back down to finish off the day.
- Need to change floors for a meeting or to see a colleague? Give the stairs a try. Even if you only go one way, it will get the blood pumping.
- Shift your seating a few times a day: Try a small object (such as a box or a book) to rest your feet on to change your posture, raise or lower your chair for a bit, move your keyboard or mouse to a different position for a small portion of your day.

Smokers Beware!

I confess. For too many years, I was a corporate smoker. I loved my cigarette break, even as I complained about the weather and being stuck outside. I learned a many things and felt a great deal of comradery with my fellow "outlaws". As a boss, I learned that employees would feel a greater bond with me over non-smoking management, often telling me things they wouldn't otherwise say about themselves, other co-workers, or bosses. As a peer, smoking gripe sessions tended to be a little more intense than ones where someone might be listening around the corner.

As an employee, my smoking bosses often felt like they could confide in me information that they might never have shared with other workers, and sometimes this information that led to my discomfort.

Yet, going on a smoke break almost always means leaving the building, and that physical removal signals to the brain that you truly are on a break. Breaks taken inside the office are often interrupted, but smoke breaks usually are not. Just be mindful that you are taking steps to make your work day more positive and don't let an angry gripe session suck you into its grasp.

Remember:

- Change your lunchtime routine
- Leave work if possible
- Take short breaks
- Shift away from work tasks during short breaks
- Move your body throughout the day
- Add the Seventh Inning Stretch
- Smokers beware

5 Meeting Busting!

Meetings can be very productive and provide a chance for everyone on a team to brainstorm, strategize, and delegate tasks. They can provide feelings of comradery and accomplishment. But let's face it, sometimes meetings can become unproductive horror shows full of pompous windbags, mean-spirited gossip, and black holes where time is stretched to epic proportions and all you want to do is get away.

The Two Factors of Meetings: Agendas and Players

Meeting agendas come in two basic varieties: determined by a player in the meeting or mandated by an authority outside the attendees. If the agenda is set by a facilitator, or player, that is present in the meeting, they set the tone and topics. If the agenda is set from an outside authority, it usually has some sort of structure or message, but the delivery is at the mercy of the facilitator.

Players come in three different varieties. There is the facilitator, who follows (or ignores) the agenda of themselves or the company. There is the team player, which is when the agenda allows open, round-table type discussions during the meeting. The passive player is more audience member than active participant, though there may be some open question and answer sessions available to the passive player.

Before the Meeting

Give yourself a time cushion so you can prepare for the meeting. Try a few arm or leg stretches as you mentally focus your attitude before you have to present your game face to the team. If you are engaged with others and they are also headed to the meeting, excuse yourself for a pre-meeting restroom break. If the herd is also headed to the restroom, try "remembering" something from your office. It's not a lie, you left your great attitude in there and you just need to pick it up beforehand. During this time, review your toolbox skills:

- Identify players
- Respond rather than react
- Identify what you can control
- Keep it private
- Attitude is a choice

If your culture welcomes it, take a beverage to the meeting. The drink can help you retain focus as well provide a socially acceptable prop to mask any facial cues you may be giving off when faced with a difficult event or revelation. This buys you time to respond rather than react.

Arrival

If your meetings are regular and the unofficial pre-meeting agenda is mean spirited, prone to spiteful gossip, or company bashing, try to arrive only a few minutes before the start. This cuts down your amount of exposure to negative energy.

If there are specific networking opportunities, you may want to arrive a little earlier. Are you are considering meeting with Human Resources about a boss, co-worker, or incident? An introduction to your HR representative, if they are at the meeting, allows you to have prior contact and boost your self-confidence. Just make sure you don't drop a bomb on them at this time or tell them that you were planning on calling/speaking with them on a matter. Lots of people keep their ears open during this time (you should to!) and you never know if the HR representative might casually ask someone if there are any issues that they might be aware of before you make the call.

When the meeting has players from other divisions or branches and you are considering a transfer, by all means, show up early, be upbeat and positive, and make those connections. Even if you haven't considered an interdepartmental transfer, you never know what opportunities may result with contact from outside your usual daily work environment.

Seating

When you have a choice, seating can make a real difference in your meeting experience.

In a team meeting, when possible, choose the seat that will present issues first or last. Minds do wander in the middle of meetings, so it's the best possible way to get your issues and agendas heard by the entire group. If there is someone who is openly mean-spirited, hostile, or dismissive of you, sit next to them. They may be comfortable calling you out on something across a table, but people often have a hard time speaking ill of someone sitting directly next to them.

If you are a passive player and the meeting is being facilitated by someone you wish to network with, sit close to the front, in the first two rows if possible. This allows you to make more eye contact and gives you a better chance of them remembering who you are.

Simple Housekeeping

Be mentally present for your meetings. Try your best to keep your mind from wandering and be respectful of those who are speaking. When engaged in active, roundtable discussions, try not to interrupt others, but make sure your own voice is heard. Mind your non-verbal cues such as eye rolls, crossed arms, or dismissive doodling. While some people actively engage their ears while doodling, they still come off as passive aggressive or dismissive. Nodding your head can show active engagement as well as assent. And while you don't have to sit there smiling like a clown, which will just make you seem insincere, a quick smile and eye contact with any new speaker shows that you are actively engaged and listening to them.

Make sure you take notes of any actionable items that you assign to others and that others assign to you. Clarify any issues or questions you may have about the tasks or assignments you pass out to others. If you are unsure in any way, touch base with the other person immediately after the meeting. Many people are simply afraid to clarify murky instructions or just decide they will figure it out later. It is much easier to approach someone about a project as soon as it is assigned.

Remember:

- Prepare your mindset
- Respond rather than react
- Calculate your arrival
- Choose your seating carefully
- Be present
- Take notes and clarify

6 When Work is Your Only Friend

Many people fall into the routine of only having friends from the workplace. After all, you spend a lot of time with these people and not all of the conversations may consist of work related items. There is a lot to gain with having a support network outside of work. Meeting new people and experiencing new things can help you focus less on any work or life problems. It can allow you to discover new opportunities, boost your self-confidence, and get a fresh perspective on life.

Sometimes, jobs end without warning. Layoffs happen. Branches close. Companies get shut down suddenly every single day. Sometimes good people make one poor choice or forget one important task or duty and lose their jobs. In today's workplace, sudden job loss is a real thing. Not to mention, often people hang on to a job longer than they should just because they like their coworkers and have no friends outside of the workplace. Sticking around because "you can't do that to your buddies" is no reason to keep yourself from seeking better opportunities or careers.

Having a social network and friends outside of your workplace, allows you to have support if you have to suddenly change careers or want to move up to something bigger and better.

If you've fallen into the trap of having only workplace friendships, how do you go about making new friends? It was much easier when we were kids, put two kids on the playground and their best buddies until it's time to go home. And college made it easy as well. Group projects, dorm rooms, and note borrowing all led us to friendships. You may have to get out of your comfort zone but there are many places to meet like-minded people.

Before you go out and seek people you have never met before, take a good look at the people you already know, but maybe haven't spoken to in a while. Have you ever had an old friend call you out of the blue just to chat and check on you? Didn't it feel great? Knowing that someone thought of you and wanted to see how you were doing made you feel pretty good. Everyone likes to be thought of and everyone likes attention. Pick up the phone and just chat or make arrangements to grab a cup of coffee or a drink if you catch them when they don't have time to speak. Make sure that you follow through with any plans. If you tell them you will call them later, do so.

Sit down and make yourself a list of five or more things you like to do, even if you haven't done them in a long time. Some examples: ride motorcycles, play a sport, build robots, watch horror films, ballroom dance, throw pottery, etc. Did you love role playing games when you were in school? There are many people that kept playing long after getting jobs and/or having families.

Once you have the list of things you like to do, write down a few more things that you have never done but always wanted to learn or do.

Now that you have a great list of interests, harness the power of the internet by putting your location and the activity into the search engine of your choice. If you can't find a club, take a class. Or call a class instructor or hobby shop and ask.

If you want to learn something new, but you aren't sure what you want to learn or do? There is an entire world of shared community workshops around the country. Many of these host different classes or events to get new enthusiasts to join their groups. There are also many shared garage space organizations for car and motorcyclist hobbyists. Look for events at any of these places and go. Remember everyone loves to talk about what they love. These places are full of people passionate about their hobbies and you may just find a hobby you love as well.

If you aren't active in your religion, you might consider finding a place of worship or community center based on your views. Once you have found a place, make sure you participate. Potluck dinners, study groups, fundraisers, and even mentoring the youth groups will help make you a part of the community and provide positive social interactions.

Consider volunteering your time and talents. So many places and agencies depend on volunteers. Love animals? Shelters need all the help they can get. Dig history? Try a senior center or history museum. Love to cook? There are plenty of places that need help making food for those less fortunate. Are you great at a sport? Adult teams are everywhere and youth organizations need all sorts of coaches and support staff.

Put on a positive attitude and make some friends outside of work. You will be glad that you did.

Remember:

- Make friends outside of work
- Reconnect with old friends
- Find hobby related organizations
- Learn a new skill
- Participate in a religious or belief based community center
- Volunteer

7 Changing Your Physical Environment

Changing your surroundings can have a positive impact on your mood and happiness. As in other areas of your job, some things you can control and other things you can't. Some workplaces allow a lot of leeway in workspace decorations, some allow no personalization at all, but give this a try to the extent that you are able. You may find that you have more control than you realize.

Take a good look around your workspace and note all the things you tend to keep at your desk or on your workspace. Is it clear, clean, and neat? Do you have piles of paperwork or memos or loose items cluttering up your space? Have you crammed too many photos onto a small wall or corner of your desk? Do you have any blank, clear space that you can see? Make note of the things that you see so often they have become a backdrop to your life.

Have you ever returned from a vacation or business trip to sigh at the state of your workspace? Was it this way before you left? Have you become accustomed to a cluttered space? If you find that work piles up while you are gone, you can simply make a plan to conquer, sort, and dispatch of the piles upon your return. If you find that this is your space, just as it is, you can make a battle plan for that as well.

Some people have vast acreage of desktop space; others feel as if they are balancing their lives on a postage stamp. Both sizes have their merits and their drawbacks. A large desk can allow for items to accumulate, which can add to frustration when searching for a specific item that you know is in there somewhere. A small desk may force you to file more things into cabinets or wall hangers, which can be just as daunting to dig through. Some clutter is digital, but can be just as intimidating to try and clear away.

Let's Get Physical

Look around and see what you use on a daily basis and what kind of storage you have available for items that you need frequently, but not constantly. If you just reached for a stapler and tried to tuck it into a desk drawer, was it easy? Was the drawer neat, orderly and accommodating or was it as messy and cluttered? Do you have shelves full of books, manuals, or binders? Are those shelves neat and organized, or are there items shoved on top of the shelved items making everything harder to access when needed? Don't get overwhelmed, you will be able to sort it all out, and chances are you have everything necessary to do so. You don't have to do everything at once. Start small and work on it one step at a time.

The Desktop

Starting with the desktop allows you immediate gratification. If you want to move items from your desktop to another area, but that other area needs organizing first, don't panic. Simply get a bin or box to store these items on a temporary basis. The program will address your temporary storage items as the last actionable item so that you will not forget them. Just make sure that you clearly mark this temporary storage so that a janitorial crew or someone else won't mistake them as recycling or trash and they get tossed or destroyed prematurely.

The multi-layer tray works wonders for paperwork. It allows you to make multiple stacks in one space that you can label for easy access. Some label ideas (customize to your personal situation):

- In (incoming items that need your attention)
- Out (outgoing items you need to pass to someone else)
- File (Items that you have finished, but need to be stored)
- High Priority
- Low Priority
- Hold (items you may need to access in the near future but may be stored after a certain time period)

You get the idea. Think about how you can classify the paperwork that comes across or stops on your workspace and get a tray that has the amount of layers that will work for your situation. If you work with large files, you may need a set of shelves as your space allows. If you only have wall space available, use vertical file holders on the wall.

Once you have your paperwork storage available, you can now begin to sort through that pile. While having an entire day to clean and sort is very gratifying, not everyone will have the luxury of doing everything at once. If that's the case, commit to spending ten minutes every day sorting your backlog of papers and set a timer.

Do you acquire and read trade journals or magazines related to your job? Clear away stacks of them into upright magazine files. Once your file is full, pull out the oldest and recycle it to make room for your newer issue. If there are articles that you wish to keep, consider cutting out the pages and dedicating a binder to these and tossing the rest into the recycling bin.

Is there a section of your desktop dedicated to personal items? Reducing your collection to only one or two inspiring things can help declutter and clear open space. If you have quite a few photos that make you happy, consider keeping only one out at a time and rotating them to make your desk feel fresh and provide constant change.

Keep it professional. Sure that "Monday's Suck" coffee mug made you laugh when you bought it and the "I owe, I owe, it's off to work I go!" mug has a ring of truth to it, but if you already get enough negativity from your job, boss, or co-workers, do you need a reminder from yourself? Opt for a plain or at least positive themed mug instead to help brighten your workspace. The same sentiment goes for any wall decorations you have accumulated. Maybe that kitten clinging on for life beneath the "Hang In There" caption gives you moral support, but consider a more professional inspirational decoration for your workspace. Avoid filling all your wall space and make sure you have plain, blank spaces on your wall to allow the eyes a rest.

The Drawers

It's okay, almost everyone has a junk drawer in their desk. We start with a few pens and some paperclips and then the next thing we know it's a treasure trove of buttons, empty mint boxes, brittle rubber bands, and pens that don't work. Now that you have your desktop under control, spend a few minutes every day working on your drawers. Toss out any pens that don't work, lose staples that have materialized, and liquid corrector fluid that has dried. Those scissors with someone else's name on it? Put them back where they belong. Once you have cleared the old items, pull everything out and wipe down the inside of the drawer with a damp cloth and allow it to dry before refilling it.

The Shelves

What kind of things (if any) do you keep on your shelves? Do you have the manuals for equipment that the company no longer has? Books that haven't been opened in a year or more? Binders and binders full of stuff from before the company went digital? Go through everything and make sure it is still needed, necessary, and relevant. Return any items that may be long to co-workers to that person and let them store it for themselves. Most equipment manuals are available online with a quick search, so if you're worried, you can do a quick search before you get rid of it.

If you find a business book that once inspired you, keep it and give it a re-read. Chances are you may remember or relearn something that once helped you or that didn't apply to your work situation then, but is relevant now.

If you are unsure if you need to keep or toss something, give it a shelf-life date of 30-90 days, 6 months, or a year to decide. Put the date into your calendar and on a sticky note on the item itself. If you reach that date and you haven't used it, throw it out!

Temporary Storage

Remember that bin you have hiding under the desk or in the corner? You know the one you used to clear your desktop before you cleaned your storage areas? Now is the time to dig it out and put things in their appropriate places. You may find that after doing without something for a long enough time, you really don't need it.

Décor

Being able to decorate your office can lift your mood and make you feel empowered. Make sure that any décor reflects the image of the company and the standards of co-workers around you. Consider who comes into your workspace before you decorate. If clients visit your office, try to project and reflect the image that they wish to see to inspire their confidence. Allow plain spaces for the eyes to rest upon and keep it uncluttered. This makes it inviting to yourself and visitors to your workspace.

If you have control over furniture placement in your office, consider re-arranging it for a fresh change. Think about your distraction levels when you choose to re-arrange. If you constantly look up every time someone walks past your open door, but you are uncomfortable sitting with your back to the door, try putting your desk to the side. You will reduce your distraction level without the worry of someone sneaking in unannounced. A fresh sightline can provide new perspectives and better moods.

We Are Living In a Digital World

Just as clutter on your desk space can compete for your attention, digital clutter can do the same to your computer screens and files. The same concepts used to streamline your physical landscape can now be utilized to clear the digital clutter of your e-world.

The Desktop

There's a reason why we call our main computer screen the desktop. It's there when you boot up and is comprised of your wallpaper and any files, folders, or application launch icons. Some companies do not allow any customization of the desktop as the information is shared between systems and users, those usually stay streamlined and somewhat clutter free. Other companies allow free reign over your digital domain where you have more control.

When you look at your computer desktop, is it as cluttered as your desk was? Consider making master folders on your desktop that matches or compliments the system you use for paperwork. If you have several projects going on at once, consider a master

"Working Projects" folder to use as a holding pen. The extra click isn't going to take much time and the clear desktop will give you a feeling of ease and control.

Consider your wallpaper. You may have a mandated plain screen, but can control the color. Pick one that energizes or soothes you since you will interact with it all day. If you are trying not to "see red" at work all day, pick a nice soothing green. If you are looking forward to your upcoming beach vacation, pick a sandy beige or watery blue. If you have a picture as your wallpaper, is it a busy picture? If it is, choose something simpler to allow the eyes a rest. Also, remember, the same rules apply to the wallpaper as to the mugs and office décor. Keep it professional.

The Other Junk Drawer

Email has certainly changed the way we communicate in our personal and professional lives. Love it or hate it, your email can turn into a digital junk drawer in no time flat. Some people hoard hundreds (or more!) of unread emails in their inbox. Some people keep even more read emails in their system.

If you have been with your company for a long time and you are allowed to use it for personal business as well as company business, make a new personal email address and direct your personal emails there. This may take quite some time considering how many things go to our email now. Emailed receipts can take the hassle out of storing bits of paper for tax time, but are they for you or your company? If they are personal business but under your work email, forward them to your personal account. Having a personal email address that you use and check often will also be essential if you decide to seek employment elsewhere.

Utilize folders in your email system. Many systems allow you to send new emails directly into your folders to keep them out of the generic inbox. These folders can help you keep track of items from important accounts, bosses, or clients. Go through your entire email inbox and clean it up. If you have mega numbers consider starting with the oldest first and commit to spending a few minutes every single day on this project. Do you really need that email from 2014? If you're not sure, make yourself a folder labeled something like "Holding" and give that folder an expiration date, just like you did items on your shelves. When that date arrives (set a reminder on your calendar) go in and delete that folder.

Make sure that you evaluate your emails as you read them. If you need to keep them, move them to the appropriate folder, but if you don't need to keep them, delete them as soon as you read them.

This may seem like something that doesn't need to be said, but it really does: Keep any digital communication professional when using your company computer or email system.

Housekeeping

Now that your office is decluttered physically and digitally, spend the last two minutes of every day on housekeeping. Put staplers and pens back into their drawers or cubbies, place paperwork back into the appropriate bins, refill your water bottle, and clean out your mug. If you have a project you absolutely need to leave directly on your desktop, slide it into a plain folder on the desktop. This leaves it readily available to you (or co-workers) but is cleaner and more pleasant. Coming in to a clear desk and a clean coffee mug makes the start of the day less stressful.

Remember:

- Conquer your desktop
- Keep it professional
- Clean any drawers
- Clear up shelving
- Revisit your temporary storage
- Declutter your digital desktop
- Clean your email
- Spend your last two minutes on housekeeping

8 Conflict Resolution

Conflict in the workplace is a given. Even friendly, happy teams experience conflict. Not all conflict is bad. Some conflicts can lead teams to discover solutions with positive results. However, conflict can also fill a team with doubts, fears, and negativity. Striving to resolve conflicts as they happen is one of the best ways to keep a positive workplace

But what is conflict? Look up the word in a dictionary and you may find the following words among the definitions:

- Struggle
- Disagreement
- Difference
- Argument
- Power
- Incompatible
- Opposing

Some people handle conflict well and as soon as it's done, forget about it. Others cannot seem to leave it behind. They may find themselves unable to understand what happened and continue to dwell upon the conflict which often results in more conflict!

So what do you do when conflict has you feeling hurt, emotional, or even bullied or you worry that you left someone with these feelings? You should see resolution.

You may be asking yourself, "Why do I have to be the one to seek resolution?" The answer is simple: The only person you can control is you. Remember the other party may not internalize the conflict at all. They may have left the conflict behind as soon as both parties walked away. So start the resolution with yourself.

Process

Give yourself time to fully process the conflict, but don't let it linger. The longer you dwell upon an incident, the more power you give it. Give yourself just enough time to make sure you are in control of your emotions, you have given thought to the other person's point of view, and you can respond rather than react. If the issue happens at the very end of business, make sure you address it as soon as you return to work the next day.

Ask yourself why you need to resolve the conflict. Do you want to dispel the negative emotions? Do you feel bad that the other person may be suffering from negative emotions even if you are not? Or do you want "the win"? Remember conflict resolution is not about who wins or loses. Conflict resolution is about removing the negativity.

Approach

Choose a positive and helpful attitude before you approach the person. Strive to be understanding. Try to give them the benefit of the doubt. Approach them in a private setting, never in front of others, and use non-aggressive language. Neutral territory is great at giving you equal footing but by approaching the other person in their own workspace, you can ease their feelings. Remember the goal is to ease any feelings of tension!

Use non-aggressive language. Try "I" phrases instead of "you" phrases. Here are some great openers that you can customize to your situation:

- I think I may have misunderstood your position on...
- Do you have a moment? I think I may have shortsighted your views on...
- I may be wrong about this...
- Can I speak to you about something that is bothering me?
- I apologize if I said (or did) something that may have hurt you...
- I'm sorry if we have gotten off on the wrong foot about...

You get the idea. Along with your "I" language, make sure you address the other party by their first name during your opening statement. If you're timid about approaching them, practice your opening statement alone before you seek them out.

Listen and then repeat what they said. This will show them that you understand their point of view rather than just being there to justify your side of things. When you show them that you understand, it is easier to disagree in a friendly manner. Remember you are striving for conflict resolution, not a win. You're not there to prove your point; you are there to dispel a negatively charged environment.

Recognize that you may not resolve the conflict, but trying is better than opting for a negatively charged atmosphere. Often a negative conflict situation isn't about the topic, but about the two (or more) egos vying for the win. Even if the resolution (or lack thereof) isn't to your liking, you have learned from the situation. Whatever the outcome, make sure you exit gracefully. Thank them for their time. If there hasn't been a resolution, leave a door open for a future positive resolution with a phrase something like this: "I will keep considering your point of view, and I would appreciate it if you would keep considering mine as well."

What if you seem to have conflict with the same person, over and over, no matter the issue? When you work in a negatively charged environment, it's easy to find yourself in repeated patterns of conflict. You can use the exact same steps to open up a dialogue about the personality differences and disagreements. You can also bring in a neutral third party to mediate the conversation.

Be Done with It

If the resolution isn't as helpful as you hoped, you need to find a way to let go of the conflict so that it doesn't become the starting point of a larger problem. When thoughts about the conflict begin to bloom in your head, deliberately shift your thoughts to another subject. Picture yourself at a favorite spot, or think about something that makes you happy. If the conflict was particularly tense, you may have to redirect your thoughts many times before you put it out of your mind altogether, but you can do it.

Learn from the situation. Too many people go into conflict resolution just to prove their own point or score a "win". It's very easy to feel almost desperate for validation when you have been working in a toxic, dysfunctional environment.

Remember:

- Resolution is about dispelling negativity, not the win
- Process the conflict from each point of view
- Be the person that seeks resolution
- Act in a timely manner
- Respond rather than react
- Approach it privately
- Use non-aggressive language
- Seek to understand
- Exit gracefully
- Do not dwell upon it

9 Bad Apples

All businesses consist of supplying a service (or product) to a customer that is delivered by employees. Employees are compensated for their time and effort. That's the black and white of it. But there's a lot of gray and hopefully some sunny yellow if the company is any good.

Good companies want good, happy employees. Good, happy employees make for good, happy customers. Unfortunately, there are plenty of managers that see only the black and white of it. Even if you work for a company with high standards and values, some managers do not reflect those values and standards. While most people identify Bad Apples as their supervisor or boss, you may find a few co-workers that are Bad Apples as well.

Extreme Bad Apple Exhibit A

Jim has worked for The Company for over ten years. During that time, Jim has seen some of his co-workers have close family members pass away. Jim knows that The Company allows time off for those individuals and sends a spray of flowers to the funerals because The Company values its employees. Jim's work buddy Adam lost his father a few months earlier and Jim had to suffer the complaints of their boss because they didn't like Adam taking the allotted bereavement time. Jim knows that The Company sent flowers to Adam's father's funeral. This puts Jim in a very tender place emotionally because Jim's his own father is terminally ill. Then three months later, Jim's father passes away. When Jim calls to inform his boss, who knew Jim's father was receiving hospice care, Jim's boss pressured Jim to come to work the next day. Jim goes in to work because he doesn't want his co-workers to hear their boss complain. When the funeral comes and goes, there is not a single flower delivered from The Company.

Extreme Bad Apple Exhibit B

Mei Lin wasn't feeling well at work, so she goes home. Later that evening, Mei Lin is in so much pain, she goes to the hospital. While in the hospital, Mei Lin was given an IV with morphine. After many long hours of doctors and tests, she is told that she needs surgery to remove her gallbladder as quickly as possible. The hospital doesn't keep her, but sends her home with a prescription for heavy pain killers and a list of surgeons to contact as soon as possible. Now it's four in the morning and Mei Lin is home and finally able to get some rest. She sets her alarm for six so that she can call her boss to inform them of the situation. Unfortunately, Mei Lin is so exhausted and full of morphine that she awakens two hours after her expected arrival time at work. She panics because she knows her boss will be angry. When Mei Lin speaks with her boss, she tries to explain that the next step is to contact a surgeon, but all her boss does is ask what time Mei Lin will be in to work.

Other Bad Apples

The No Sick Time Bad Apple: The boss that whines and complains when someone has to miss work due to being ill. Sure, it can be a hardship when someone is out sick, but it can be a hardship when they come to work and spread the illness to others and then everyone is out sick.

The No Children Bad Apple: The boss that is uncaring and rude when you have to miss work due to a sick child or any of the other unexpected crisis situations that come with having kids.

The Glory Claimer Bad Apple: The boss that takes all the credit for everything, never acknowledging the success of the team, even if one person had the brilliant thought or breakthrough that led to the success.

The Finger Pointer Bad Apple: The boss that can never face up to their own mistakes, or if the team makes a mistake, can't take the credit for allowing it to happen. They play their own version of Pin the Tail on the Donkey whenever something goes wrong.

The Information Hoarder Bad Apple: The boss that keeps control and power by never sharing vital information, therefore making their own team look inept or allowing them to make critical errors in their work.

The Micro Bad Apple: The boss that micromanages every task, slowing down the process and eroding trust.

The Flat Out Jerk Bad Apple: The mean spirited boss that speaks ill of others, possibly even when they are present. They may be sexist, racist, or simply mean, sometimes all three. Usually the Flat Out Jerk is a combination of many Bad Apple types.

The Bumbling Bad Apple: The boss that is just a mess. Undisciplined, unorganized, untrained, and/or inept, this boss may have a heart of gold, but the lack of leadership and people skills can leave a team in real trouble.

The Workaholic Bad Apple: The boss that spends every single moment of their lives focused on work and expects you to as well.

There are many, many other Bad Apples out there. Most Bad Apples often display traits from several of the Bad Apple varieties.

What Can You Do

So what can you do about a Bad Apple? Sometimes just knowing the Bad Apple is going to be a Bad Apple allows you to put things in perspective so you can respond rather than react. You can try a speaking to the Bad Apple and let them know how you feel. Don't expect a huge outpouring of emotion or remorse because most Bad Apples are that way because of their poor people skills. You can try ignoring the negativity of the Bad Apple and try to get along. Sometimes you need to go above the Bad Apple's head, if that option exists. If you work for a Bad Apple that is the top boss, you need to decide if your career with that company is worth the negative treatment.

While you are deciding on what to do with your Bad Apple, here are some things you should be doing:

- Document actionable items and communications as often as possible by saving emails, reports, and memos.
- Be very professional in your own work and behavior.
- Keep a diary- make it straightforward, strictly factual, date and time of behavior witnessed and the names witnesses (if any)
- Keep these actions to yourself

If you decide to have an open dialogue, similar to a conflict resolution visit. Make sure you plan it out and keep your emotions in check. Don't call them out in front of teammates. Choose only one or two items to focus on during the conversation. Keep these one or two items in front of you on a piece of paper and list examples and specific incidents. Go in to the meeting with open expectations. Even if the meeting appears to go your way, make sure you document your meeting in your work diary with as much detail as you can recall.

If you feel as if there is no way to have this open dialogue with your Bad Apple, consult your company's human resources manual or speak to your boss's boss. You have to make the choice to live with your Bad Apple, report the Bad Apple, or leave the job. If you leave the job, you may still choose to report the Bad Apple or if your company has an exit interview, be honest.

If you work at a small company and the Bad Apple is the only boss or owner, you can either opt for an open dialogue, live with it, or leave.

Sometimes a co-worker or peer is the Bad Apple that spoils the barrel. In that case, you can choose to have an open dialogue with that person, report that person, or choose to live with that person.

Most people spend close to 70% of their time at work. Doing nothing is a choice to live with the situation. If you work for or with a Bad Apple, you can ignore it, do something about it, or find a Happy Apple at another branch or company.

Businesses run on people. They shouldn't run over people.

Remember:

- Recognize the Bad Apple
- Keep it private
- Save emails, memos, and reports
- Keep a work diary
- Be professional in your actions and behavior
- Decide what action you will take
- Doing nothing is an action

10 When Enough is Enough (And even when it isn't!)

Warning: If you decide to seek other employment, be very careful about sharing this information with co-workers. Negative workplaces often thrive on gossip as a commodity of power.

The Big Question

Should you stay or should you go? It can be the easiest question or the hardest. Sometimes, the answer is leave, even if you love your job. There are few questions we ask of ourselves that have as much power over our lives than that of changing jobs or careers. One person may have a quick, concise reason to stay and another may see the handwriting on the wall, so to speak. To one person, the job may just be a job, to another it might be an identity, a labor of love, and the product of years of dedication and hard work.

Why People Stay

Let's look at all the reasons people stay at a job they hate:

- Financial stability
- Health benefits
- Nearing retirement age
- Corporate discounts or perks
- Love of the job
- Comradery at work
- Seniority
- Habit/Familiarity
- Customer relationships
- Unemployment rates
- Fear
- Location

Let's take a closer look, as some of these reasons are very valid.

If you are less than a year or two from retirement with a company you have given many years of service to, it may be in your best long-term interest (unless the stress is affecting you physically) to stay. You may find that working the program can provide you the changes and will to carry on until retirement day.

If you, or one of your beneficiaries, is having health difficulties with a long term illness or condition, it may be wise to stay with the company and not have to worry about the potential changes to health insurance premiums, deductibles, co-pays, or possibly having to change health care providers during this time.

Benefits or discounts can vary wildly between companies and be very specialized. One person may receive free or super-reduced tuition to a college or university for themselves or their children. Another person may work for an airline that provides free travel and has family that they frequently visit, such as an older parent or a college aged child.

Love of the job can be very powerful. Many, many people are in love with their job while they are being strangled by their coworkers or bosses. They find fulfillment with their customers and daily routines and it can be a very good thing. However, a few Bad Apples can indeed spoil the barrel.

You may already know that your time with your company is coming to a close. You may have even known it before you chose this program. You may have chosen to work the program just to help you shake off the negativity of your work environment long enough to find other employment. If you have made this decision, please continue to work the program for as long as you are with your current job, especially if you find you have a bitter taste in your mouth. Continue to work it through your entire last day. Allow your feelings of relief to further boost your mental health and wellbeing. There's nothing better than a graceful exit.

If you are unsure, or on the fence, here's a well-known secret that people rarely utilize: You don't have to be unemployed to look for another job. You don't even have to accept a job offer when it comes your way. Truth is the future is always uncertain. Job's end suddenly all the time. Layoffs happen, companies close, branches get eliminated. It's always a great idea to keep an updated resume on hand and keep your interview skills sharp. Working on your resume once a year and reading a few articles on current interviewing trends can give you a clear perspective of the work you do and value you provide to your current employer. Being offered a job that you do not have to take can give you a feeling of empowerment and control.

If you haven't looked for a job in a while (or decades) make sure you do your research on the brave new world out there. Create (or re-evaluate) your LinkedIn profile. Don't underestimate LinkedIn as a "professional Facebook." A great profile with a professional photo and relevant information can help you get noticed by recruiters. . There are many articles on the internet that can help you create a profile that recruiters will notice. And even with a killer LinkedIn profile, make sure you update your resume as some people still like to see a hardcopy of a resume. Spend some time reading articles on using LinkedIn and creating your resume. There is a plethora of information available using any search engine you prefer. Ensure that you use your personal email address instead of your work email address on applications, resumes and LinkedIn contact.

When job hunting, make sure you keep a positive, upbeat attitude when speaking of your current employer. Seek the aid of the internet to see what questions you may face and practice how to tactfully, respectfully speak about your current work situation, even if you hate it.

Humans are complex beings with complex emotions, make sure you don't miss out on better opportunities in life just because you don't know what's out there or fear change.

And this deserves another mention:

* Warning: If you decide to seek other employment, be very careful about sharing this information with co-workers. Negative workplaces often thrive on gossip as a commodity of power.

Remember:

- You don't have to decide to leave to seek potential opportunities
- Update your resume annually
- Create and update your LinkedIn profile
- Research interview trends
- Exit gracefully

ABOUT THE AUTHOR

Susie Stone is an author and entrepreneur living in Southwest Florida with her husband, son, and various furry beasts. When not writing or working, she is out exploring her community, beachcombing for shells and sea glass, and playing the ukulele. She is still trying to conquer the Zen of always having sand in the car. Look for her online course coming to Udemy in the fall of 2016.

61166233R00036

Made in the USA
Lexington, KY
02 March 2017